THE GREATNESS OF DADS

THE GREAT- NESS OF DADS

Kirsten Matthew

CHRONICLE BOOKS

SAN FRANCISCO

For my dad, Robert Harry Matthew.
And for Marc's Sofia and Tommy.

Contents

Introduction

On Sundays, I'd often go to work with my dad. It was a way for my mum, who was with me and my sister all week, to get a break, and for us to spend some time with the man who got home well after we went to bed most nights.

At his office in the city, we'd run through the quiet hallways, play on the typewriters, and pocket pieces of stationery from the secretaries' desks. Dad would disappear behind his office door . . . but he was there. I'd type him notes, run down the hallway, and slip them under the door.

It wasn't always easy to have a dad who worked so hard. He didn't make it to parent-teacher conferences or ballet recitals (the one time he made it to a show–an eleventh-hour arrival that meant he stood watching from the wings–I thought my heart would burst with happiness). On rare holidays away together, he'd be someone I needed to get to know all over again.

But there were and are wonderful things about my dad, Robert Harry Matthew. He gave us luxuries he didn't get as a child: a middle-class upbringing; a university education; endless encouragement. From him, I learned to question authority, to always be reading, and that, as he loves to say ad nauseam, "Girls can do anything." He taught me to never leave the party first, to love people for who they are, to treat friends as family, and to be loyal to the bitter end.

By the time we were teenagers, Dad had more time to be with us, and I became his confidante, his friend, and, along with my sister, his pride and joy. We've danced together, traveled together, and got through family crises together. We've argued and disagreed with each other. On many nights in my twenties and thirties, we sat up playing cards and listening to music until 3 a.m. These days, we have early dinners and talk politics and books. He's beloved by my friends, the smartest person I know, and still the most important man in my life.

What I've discovered from talking to fathers and children from all walks of life and from all over the world is that everyone's relationship with their dad is complicated. That's the way it should be–it's the meaning and the nature of the ties that bind us to our parents. And that's really where the motivation for this book came from. There are many books about dads already, and just as many that I couldn't or wouldn't buy my dad because the schmaltz would turn him off. I wanted to make a book that celebrates dads in a realistic, nuanced, everyday way. The result is this, *The Greatness of Dads*.

I can't claim that the idea for this book is entirely my own. It came, initially, from my friend of thirty years, Marc Ellis (see his interview on page 138). He's a dad too–to Tommy and Sofia–and this book is partly for them.

The chapters in this book follow the trajectory of our lifetimes with our dads–from birth to adulthood. They extol the things that dads do so well, and reflect on some of the things they might not (like dressing and dancing). There are pearls of wisdom from dads past and present, and some really good (and really weird) pieces of dad advice.

For the record, my dad has always been a snappy dresser and is a very good dancer, but he did, for many years, sport quite a bad comb-over (see left). His taste in music leans toward classic hits and country and western, and his advice is often as poetic as the lyrics of the songs he loves. I'm glad he's my dad.

Kirsten Matthew

Young Love

A baby will make love stronger, days shorter, nights longer, bankroll smaller, home happier, clothes shabbier, the past forgotten, and the future worth living for.

Anonymous

You don't have to be the best dad in the world; you have to be her dad. You have to be the goofy, awkward guy that everyone falls in love with. It's OK to have days where you feel like you can't hack it, or think that everyone else has it together except you; to have no idea what you're doing; to make it up as you go along.

Allison Robicelli

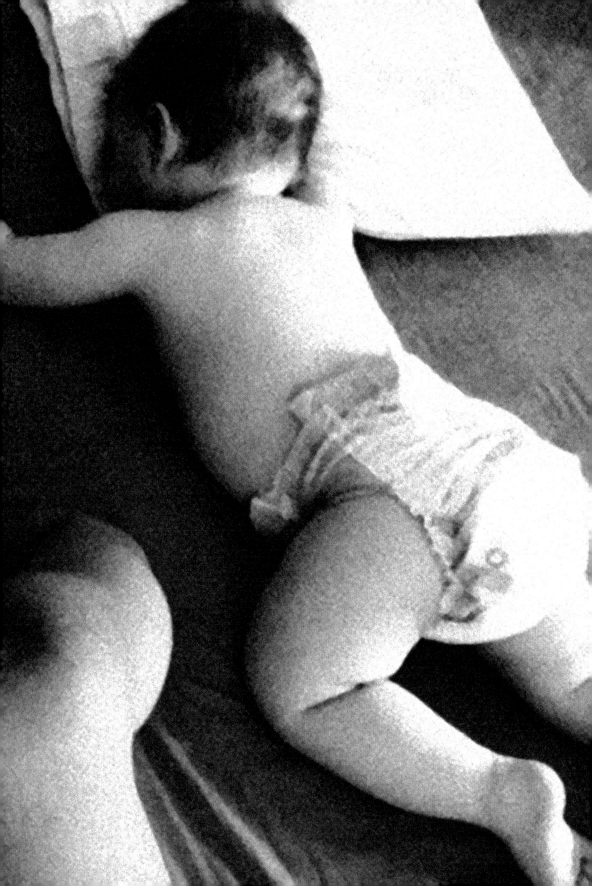

Father

He never made a fortune, or a noise
In the world where men are seeking after fame;
But he had a healthy brood of girls and boys
Who loved the very ground on which he trod
They thought him just little short of God;
Oh you should have heard the way they said his name
—"Father."

Ella Wheeler Wilcox

The first conscious parental thought I ever had—cradling my bawling three-week-old son in my arms and staring out the window at the gray light crawling over the horizon—was, "OK. Don't kill the baby."

Greg Knauss

I cannot think of any need
in childhood as strong
as the need for a father's
protection.

Sigmund Freud

A man is not complete until he has seen the baby he has made.

Sammy Davis Jr.

Mayra Armstrong

41, real estate manager, Apex, North Carolina, USA

My dad, Dr. Jose Alejo Garza, was born and raised in Monterrey, Mexico. He is a character and has some very funny stories about growing up in Mexico. He'll tell you how he used to eat weird things, anything that could fit in a pot, including toads, at his dad's ranch. They didn't have a lot of money—as a kid, when he'd give a present at a birthday party, he'd only be able to give a tube of toothpaste or a bar of soap. He didn't get to travel with his family.

He came to the USA—after he finished medical school in 1973—with a dictionary because he didn't speak proper English. He went to school, worked hard, did a year in the air force. He gets offended when people criticize Mexican immigrants, because he worked hard. He says he did it the right way, and he's proud of everything he's accomplished.

He was a very good doctor, but he's seventy-one and retired now. He did open-heart and brain surgery anesthesia. My mother and he got together in Mexico. They have been married for forty-one years and live in San Antonio, Texas.

Ours was a very traditional childhood. My dad was very strict, Mexican macho style. I have two sisters and one brother and we had to follow the rules. Everything had to be clean and in its place—no feet on the sofa, no handprints on sliding doors. We had to do chores, earn our money. We had to come home on time; we had to finish university or we couldn't live under his roof; and there were no tattoos or piercings allowed. They were just the rules. I was the black sheep and got in trouble the most; I guess I was the rebel in the family.

I can't say it was perfect, with no ups and downs, but we had horses, dogs, and ducks. We lived on two-and-a-half acres, with stables, and we took riding lessons because my dad loves horses. We each got a car on our sixteenth birthday. I went to Europe for two months for my quinceañera.

He always told me to marry someone at least six years older than me; I don't know why. But my husband is six years older than me. I met him when I went to visit my uncle in Hong Kong. We have two kids: Alec, who is eight, and Milla, who is six.

I think it's thanks to my father's hard work and strict rules that I am a good parent today. My children

He's very spontaneous. He's capsized boats; he got his license to fly a plane. He told my mom he was going for coffee once and came back with a motorcycle and a Maserati.

knew from an early age how important it is to study and that they are expected to go to university. I think it is very important to set rules and to be respectful, to not talk back, to come home when you are supposed to. My husband, John, is a lot more relaxed.

Dad is a lot more relaxed now too. My mom has taught him to enjoy things. He's very spontaneous. He's capsized boats; he got his license to fly a plane. He told my mom he was going for coffee once and came back with a motorcycle and a Maserati. Until a few years ago, he would water-ski on one ski. I am surprised he still has all of his fingers and toes. He keeps busy with numerous hobbies—fishing, traveling—and was flying his plane until last year. And he is a fantastic grandparent. He visits us often and does so many things for the kids. My mother has told me that he does things for my kids that he never did for us— changing diapers, helping with baths— because he was always working. Now he reads the news from Mexico on his iPad every morning when he has his coffee, helps around the house, and is a very happy grandfather.

Daddy's Girl

Alas, raising a young lady is a mystery even beyond an enchanter's skill.

Lloyd Alexander, from *The Castle of Llyr*

In our household, I'd been assigned Daddy's sidekick. Starting as a
toddler, I'd kept a place standing beside him in his truck, and for the rest
of his days, his lanky arm still reflexively extended itself at stop
signs, as if to stop a smaller me from pitching through the windshield.

. . . Without Daddy, the wide plain of Minnesota was a vast and empty
canvas, me a flealike pin dot scurrying across.

Mary Karr

Dear Malia and Sasha,

When I was a young man, I thought life was all about me—about how I'd make
my way in the world, become successful, and get the things I want. But
then the two of you came into my world with all your curiosity and mischief
and those smiles that never fail to fill my heart and light up my day. And
suddenly, all my big plans for myself didn't seem so important anymore.
I soon found that the greatest joy in my life was the joy I saw in yours.
And I realized that my own life wouldn't count for much unless I was able
to ensure that you had every opportunity for happiness and fulfillment in
yours. In the end, girls, that's why I ran for President: because of what
I want for you and for every child in this nation . . .

    These are the things I want for you—to grow up in a world with no limits
on your dreams and no achievements beyond your reach, and to grow into

compassionate, committed women who will help build that world. And
I want every child to have the same chances to learn and dream and grow
and thrive that you girls have. That's why I've taken our family on this
great adventure. I am so proud of both of you. I love you more than you
can ever know. And I am grateful every day for your patience, poise, grace,
and humor as we prepare to start our new life together in the White House.

Love, Dad

**Barack Obama in an open letter to his daughters, Malia and Sasha,
written in 2009 prior to his inauguration**

He was an excellent whistler, the kind
who can whistle through his teeth.
He drummed on the steering wheel
while he drove, and played Jim Croce's
Greatest Hits tape over and over.
If it was dark when we pulled in the
driveway, I would pretend to be asleep
so he would carry me inside.

Margaret Mason

When it comes
to men who are
romantically
interested in you,
it's really simple.
Just ignore
everything they
say and only pay
attention to what
they do.

Randy Pausch

He was interested in absolutely everything we did, and it didn't make any difference that we were girls.

Una Hobday

The father of a daughter is nothing but a high-class hostage. A father turns a stony face to his sons, berates them, shakes his antlers, paws the ground, snorts, runs them off into the underbrush, but when his daughter puts her arm over his shoulder and says, "Daddy, I need to ask you something," he is a pat of butter in a hot frying pan.

Garrison Keillor

Dear Pie . . .

```
Worry about courage
Worry about cleanliness
Worry about efficiency
Worry about horsemanship
Worry about . . .

Don't worry about popular opinion
Don't worry about dolls
Don't worry about the past
Don't worry about the future
Don't worry about growing up
Don't worry about anybody getting ahead of you
Don't worry about triumph
Don't worry about failure unless it comes through your own fault
Don't worry about mosquitoes
Don't worry about flies
Don't worry about insects in general
Don't worry about parents
Don't worry about boys
Don't worry about disappointments
Don't worry about pleasures
Don't worry about satisfactions
```

F. Scott Fitzgerald to his daughter, Scottie, in 1933

To be the father of growing daughters is to understand something of what Yeats evokes with his imperishable phrase "terrible beauty." Nothing can make one so happily exhilarated or so frightened; it's a solid lesson in the limitations of self to realize that your heart is running around inside someone else's body.

Christopher Hitchens

Things my father taught me that stuck: How to hit the baseball off the T. All the parts under the hood of my first car. How to appreciate *The Muppet Show*. Never bring home any bikers. That I don't answer to a horn honk: that boy had better come to the door.

Sarah Brown

Natalia Fedner

32, fashion designer, Los Angeles, California, USA

I immigrated to Columbus, Ohio, from Chernivtsi, Ukraine (the former USSR), with my mother and my father, Gregory Fedner, in 1988. He was twenty-eight years old when we came to America. He's a civil engineer.

We had to leave the USSR as refugees, which meant a long journey and stays in several European countries along the way. We lived in the small seaside town of Ladispoli in Italy. I was five years old and remember being very, very scared of the sea, only going in as far as my ankles because I was convinced I would be swept away by a wave. My father, on the other hand, took great delight in disappearing beyond the horizon. He would bring me beautiful seashells from his adventures; I had a whole bag of them by the end of our three-month stay. We were poor—we couldn't take much of anything with us when we left the USSR. Any money or jewelry would have been stolen or confiscated, so the only things we could bring were tchotchkes, like decorated wooden spoons, and *matryoshki* (nesting dolls). So we sold these at the Roman market to make money while we waited to hear about our visa status. I remember being at the market with my parents and I was never happier. It was such a pleasure.

The year I was fourteen, I spent Halloween night passing out candy with my father in Columbus, Ohio, while my mom took my five-year-old twin sisters trick-or-treating. We bought quite a lot of candy (and not just Tootsie Rolls, but the good, expensive chocolate bars). Kids started ringing the doorbell, and my dad and I took turns handing out the candy. I noticed he was giving them whole handfuls. I scolded him not to or else we would run out of candy before we ran out of trick-or-treaters. He told me that when he was a child in Ukraine they didn't have holidays like Halloween. They had tanks and soldiers that marched down the streets. He said when he saw the amount of joy in those children's eyes at getting the candy he wished he could have experienced that as a kid. So I started giving out handfuls too. And, when we ran out of candy, we ran to the local grocery store to get more.

As a teenager, there were a lot of hard conversations—too many to recollect really. My dad and I did not get along. It may sound silly now, but the hardest conversations were about my room and how messy it was. It would drive him crazy and cause all sorts of fights with my mother. For him, it didn't matter that my grades were perfect—if my room was a mess, in his eyes, I was a mess. But, for me, it was just a room. Luckily, once I moved out we were able to become friends.

His favorite place? Probably his study. It's his sanctuary away from a house full of women. He's a collector of World War II documents: bank notes, passports, journals, all sorts of SS items. He collects these items because he believes their historical significance is very important and must not be forgotten.

I think emigrating was the bravest thing Dad ever did. It took all his courage and now he is a lot more risk averse. He really appreciates the USA

I think emigrating was the bravest thing Dad ever did.
It took all his courage . . .

and how much opportunity it has given both his offspring and his mother, who immigrated a few years after us. It also puts into perspective just how bad he had it growing up in the USSR, so he is very proud to be an American and a capitalist. He mistrusts anything that borders on communism because he lived through the ravages of the system. He's never been back to the Ukraine because of how horrible it was for us and our ancestors.

My dad wanted me to have a stable job, so he was not exactly happy when I took my perfect grades to art school rather than to an Ivy League university. He had advised me to become a doctor or a lawyer, something that would give me financial security. Two art degrees later and as the owner of a successful fashion line, I'm really glad I didn't listen to him. I love that my job is my love. And my dad admitted he was wrong after Jennifer Lopez wore one of my designs. He said that he was proud of the risks I had taken and that I hadn't listened to all his warnings. I still take lots of career risks and I'm glad to know I have his approval.

Boys Will Be Boys

Lately all my friends are worried that they're turning into their fathers. I'm worried that I'm not.

Dan Zevin

My dad never grew out of his upbringing. He worked hard when he was a kid. He worked in the soil with his hands and sang gospel music, the very stuff of the American earth, and that's who he was, and he never lost that. And that stayed with me. The fact that he was such an iconic figure and praised highly by so many people, but he was not haughty and puffed up, that he was down to earth. That mattered. Kindness. He was a kind man, he was a gentle and loving man. That's what endures. He was never angry, he was never forceful, he was always peaceful within his nature, and that's what lasts. It's what remains in the heart. A lot of people remember the darkness, or the sadness, the Man in Black. Well, there's so much more to who he was. He was asked by Larry King what he would like to most be remembered as, and he said, "A good father." And in that he's very successful.

John Carter Cash on his father, Johnny Cash

I never saw my dad cry. My son saw me cry. My dad never told me he loved me, and consequently I told Scott I loved him every other minute. The point is, I'll make less mistakes than my dad, my sons hopefully will make less mistakes than me, and their sons will make less mistakes than their dads.

James Caan

When I was seven, he told everybody that, one day, I would be number one.

It actually is quite simple: my father is a man who didn't have choice in his own life. And, as a result, he wanted to give us the one thing he could: freedom for us to choose our life by giving us the American Dream. He associated choice with economics, and he wanted the fastest road to the American Dream for his kids.

Andre Agassi

I stumbled in his hob-nailed wake,
Fell sometimes on the polished sod;
Sometimes he rode me on his back
Dipping and rising to his plod.

I wanted to grow up and plough,
To close one eye, stiffen my arm.
All I ever did was follow
In his broad shadow round the farm.

Seamus Heaney, from "Follower"

No relationship has more power than the one between a father and son. A man may be closer to his mother, have more impassioned rivalries with his brother, love his wife more desperately. But father and son–whether for good or for ill–that relationship molds a man. A son sees in his father achievement, mastery–all the things he hopes to be. A father sees in his son potential, the possibility of all the things he has not done and may never do.

David Granger

Do I want to be a hero to my son? No. I would like to be a very real human being. That's hard enough.

Robert Downey Jr.

Things you'll never
regret doing: visiting your
grandmother, standing up to
a bully, skydiving, living in
Paris, falling madly in love.

Sam de Brito

My father's car is marooned in a quagmire, miles up a dirt track in remote Berkshire countryside. Dad stands beside it, having abandoned the fruitless task of exhuming it from its boggy grave. He is beaming.

It is my twelfth birthday and he has contrived this adventure as a special treat for me. He has driven the family saloon as if it were an Army jeep, miles off-piste and into the mud on purpose. I am at his side, his conspirator in the mischief, and of course I am delighted.

We both know what will happen next. Dad and I will trek back to our village–it's 1964; mobile phones have yet to be invented–and call on Major Staples. The Major, who is bluff, kind, and as practical as Dad is useless at anything manual, will be induced to drive out with tow rope and toolbox to rescue us.

There will be a drama and that will perk Dad up no end. After we're unstuck, Dad and I will drive off–sometimes, in fact, he'll let me drive along the track, because this is the era before health and safety blighted our fun–and then go for a meal at our favorite transport café.

Charlie Mortimer

Massachusetts-based artist and graphic designer David Laferriere draws original illustrations on his sons' sandwich bags every school day. He's been doing it for over eight years and has created over a thousand different illustrations. "They love it," he says, "and nothing makes me happier than hearing their reaction at the end of the day."

Of all nature's gifts to the human race,
what is sweeter to a father than his children?

Marcus Tullius Cicero

I hope that he will have none of my smaller and undesirable qualities and all of my better ones. I want him to grow into a man who is unplagued, regarded affectionately for his sensitivity and intelligence and candor and steadfastness and a tranquillity at the heart of his being that comes from knowing that he has been loved, that he has no obligation to carry forth a family myth, that he is unencumbered. And that he will value the company of his mother and father because he feels it is uncomplicated by our insistence that he abandon his identity for one we need him to embrace.

Alec Wilkinson

Garth Callaghan

46, creator of Napkin Notes, *Glen Allen, Virginia, USA*

For all intents and purposes, I'm dying. My prognosis is that I'm never going to be cured — it's really simple. I have kidney cancer.

I have one daughter, Emma. I started writing notes and putting them in her lunch when she was in kindergarten. It wasn't a thing. It wasn't a habit, for sure. They started out simply — 'Have a good day', 'I love you' — but, when Emma was in sixth grade, I was diagnosed with cancer for the first time. I started to make the notes more mature, more inspirational, more motivational. Emma started saving the notes.

If I were to be honest, I did it so that she might love me a little more than she loved her mum. I'd been the one who had gone out to work every day and I was incredibly jealous of the time my wife spent with Emma at home. When Emma was in second or third grade, my wife started working at the school. I became the de facto lunch guy.

When I was diagnosed with cancer for the third time, I read about a social movement called Because I Said I Would. It's all about making promises and keeping them. All I could think about was the implied promise to my daughter that I'd always be here. So I made a promise to write out enough notes for every day. I contacted the person behind the social movement and the local paper did a story.

Next thing my phone was ringing off the hook. In hindsight, I really wasn't prepared, but that's when publishers got in touch, movie studios, all within five days of the

Napkin Notes breaking on the internet. I'm just a dad who writes on a piece of paper, and everybody can do that, but it's because I have cancer that the story resonates.

The book *Napkin Notes* was published in October 2015 in the US and has been translated into Italian, Portuguese, Korean, Japanese, Italian, Chinese and Russian. Reese Witherspoon is producing the movie. Ninety nine per cent of our lives are still normal, but one per cent is just crazy.

Having a girl gives you the best of both worlds — it's the ultimate experience in being a dad. I want Emma to grow up to be strong and confident and to look to herself for strength first. The notes are geared towards her reaching that.

We have an open, honest relationship. Any conversation that starts with 'I have cancer', is difficult. She was eleven the first time I had to explain what cancer was. However, I have never, and will never, correct her when she says, 'My dad's going to beat this.'

We're both very comfortable in our own skin and we don't really care what the outside world thinks. We both like science fiction and have sarcastic senses of humour. I'm teaching her to drive now, and spending that time with someone with a similar mindset is remarkable. We have inside jokes without even knowing we have them. We can convey volumes in five words or less. I don't have that with my wife. We just have that with each other.

My dad, Stephen Callaghan, did not communicate well and didn't know how to build up his kids. He came from

a close-knit family of Irish Catholics and there were seven kids. He didn't have a very good role model for a father, but he did his best to be a dad.

He was the local mortician in a small town of 670 people, and I grew up in a funeral home. I was expected to help out in the business. Some jobs were not cool, like washing the hearse. I realise, as a grown-up, that it wasn't just about the job — it was about respect for the families whose family member had died.

He wasn't particularly busy. He only worked a hundred days a year, so he was present most times. There were times I could tell he loved being a dad and times he was just going through the motions. He hated going to our high-school band concerts. He went begrudgingly while my mum went with enthusiasm.

He passed away before my first cancer diagnosis, but before that, when he'd visit us, we'd do projects on the house together. My dad was really good at that stuff and took the time to teach it. He enjoyed doing it. I don't enjoy it, and I'm not good at it either. But I have a lot of his old tools.

My dad was a much better grand-father than a father. When he came to stay he would get down on the floor with Emma or into her little princess tent. He loved being a grandfather and revelled in that role. As a grandfather, you have all the time in the world.

Post-cancer, I don't dwell on my mortality, but I can't watch a wedding video or think about my own grandchildren. I can think about today and tomorrow and next week and next year, but when I think about Emma as a grown-up who gets married and has kids — well, I just can't. If I'm lucky enough to make it to my sixties, I hope I can sit back and really relax and enjoy the time I have with my daughter and my grandkids. But the factual part of me recognises that is not going to happen for me. Emma says, 'My dad's going to beat this', but do you know what? I'm not. And that breaks my heart.

It Runs in the Family

The family, that dear octopus from whose tentacles we never quite escape, nor in our innermost hearts ever quite wish to.

Dodie Smith

My father had a profound influence
on me–he was a lunatic.

Spike Milligan

All of the good bits of me as a father come from the role model I've had, and, honestly, I think he's a pretty hard act to follow.

Geoff Blackwell

I learned that work can be
meaningful from my father.
Everything he does–from his most
complex academic mathematics to
digging in the garden–he tackles
with joy and resolve and enthusiasm.
My earliest memories of my father
are of seeing him work at his desk
and realizing that he was happy.
I did not know it then, but that was
one of the most precious gifts a
father can give his child.

Malcolm Gladwell

"Why do men like me want sons?" he wondered. "It must be because they hope in their poor beaten souls that these new men, who are their blood, will do the things they were not strong enough nor wise enough nor brave enough to do. It is rather like another chance with life; like a new bag of coins at a table of luck after your fortune is gone."

Old Robert in John Steinbeck's _Cup of Gold_

Lovely walk this morning with Father, who grows old with a very graceful philosophy. Comparing bees and butterflies to elephants & parrots & speaking of indentures with the leveller. Barging through the hedges and over the walls with the help of my shoulder, blaspheming and stopping to rest under color of admiring the view. I'll never have anyone like him.

Samuel Beckett, to a friend, 1933

One of the greatest gifts my father gave me–unintentionally–was witnessing the courage with which he bore adversity. We had a bit of a roller-coaster life with some really challenging financial periods. He was always unshaken, completely tranquil, the same ebullient, laughing, jovial man.

Ben Okri

Every time I buy chips
I think of my father.

Roddy Doyle

*Driving down a nice two-lane highway, summer day, Ann Arbor, Michigan.
I'm in the backseat of a '49 Cadillac. Always had a good car, my dad.
Frank Sinatra's singing: "Fairy tales can come true / It can happen to you /
If you're young at heart." My dad's singing along. From that moment on,
when people asked me what I wanted to be, I would say, "A singer."*

Iggy Pop

Kirsten Fleming

37, journalist, New York City, USA

I grew up in Jackson, New Jersey, and I live in Manhattan but my dad, Andrew Joseph Fleming, was from the Bronx. He was a complicated man who grew up with an alcoholic father, and he did everything in his power to provide the childhood he never had. He died eight years ago, at fifty-nine.

He was tough but attentive. He loved sports and made sure we did too. But he was a stubborn bastard. Once a pizzeria sent him the wrong order and, when they didn't offer to fix it, he slapped "The Ban" on that pizzeria. As a family we could never go there again. We called him Dandy Andy because he was the opposite of light and dandy. He could be cranky as all hell.

I was a teenage athlete and played basketball and soccer during my high-school years. My friends told me to try out for cheerleading because I could jump. When I told him I was going to be a cheerleader, he told me that I "had rocks in my head" and should go out for cross-country instead. I went out for cross-country and became an obsessive long-distance runner. When I was really little, he would jog a few miles to keep in shape and I would try to keep up with him. So, when he forced me to run cross-country, I had no idea I would become a runner. When I crossed the finish line of my first marathon in 2002, he was there beaming and taking photos. He grinned like a clown. He was so proud. And he knew he was the reason I became a runner in the first place. He let me lean on him as we walked around the field together afterward, keeping me loose as I cooled down. There was no one else I wanted to share that moment with.

He gave bad advice too. When I quit my job in Boston and my best friend and I went to Costa Rica for a month, he didn't talk to me for weeks; he thought it was terrible that I traveled without a job. But I learned so much about myself and figured out that I wanted to write for a living.

When my father was diagnosed with terminal cancer, he didn't want to talk at all. But he started his chemotherapy in December, and at Christmas he and I stayed up late at night watching a John Wayne marathon including *The Shootist*, which is about a terminally ill man going out on his terms. He told me how chemo wasn't that bad and he felt like he was going to live for a while. I know he hadn't really opened up to anyone so, as much as it was painful to talk about, I was happy he did.

We called him Dandy Andy because he was the opposite of light and dandy. He could be cranky as all hell.

Dressed to the Nines

Every dad is entitled to one hideous shirt and one horrible sweater. It's part of the dad code.

Tom Baker in *Cheaper by the Dozen 2*

He was dressed in his standard around-the-house outfit, which is to say, his underpants. No matter the season, he wore them without a shirt or socks, the way a toddler might pad about in a diaper. For as long as any of us could remember, this was the way it went: he returned home from work and stepped out of his slacks, sighing with relief, as if they were oppressive, like high heels. All said, my father looked good in his underpants, better than the guys in the Penney's catalog, who were, in my opinion, consistently weak in the leg department. Silhouetted in the doorway, he resembled a wrestler.

David Sedaris, "Laugh, Kookaburra"

If I can walk around in my underwear and pull them up super high so that it's just gross-looking and then try to be very serious with them, I like to do that . . .

Paul Rudd

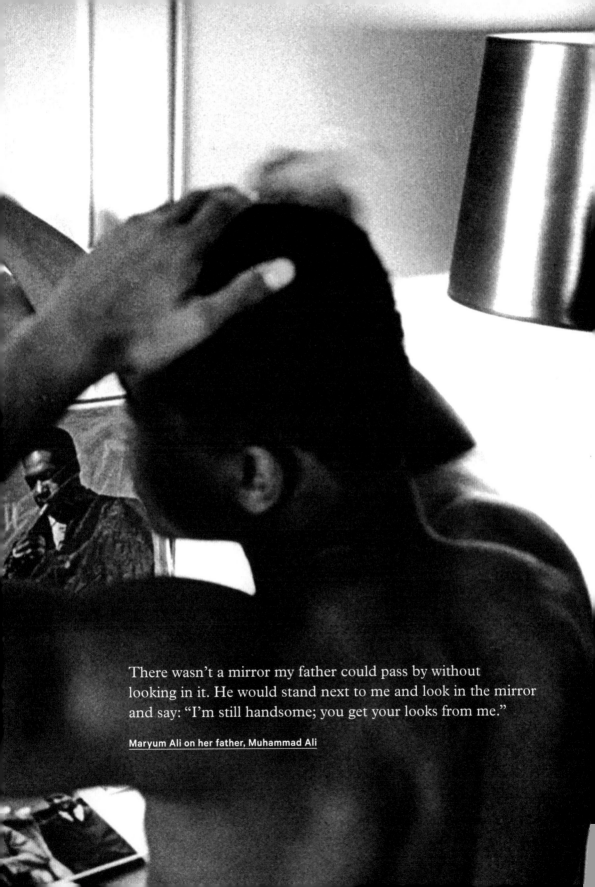

There wasn't a mirror my father could pass by without looking in it. He would stand next to me and look in the mirror and say: "I'm still handsome; you get your looks from me."

Maryum Ali on her father, Muhammad Ali

When I was about twelve and first started wearing lipstick, my dad would ask, "Are you wearing makeup?" I would say back, "You're wearing more makeup there than I am!"

Georgia May Jagger on her father, Mick Jagger

Few men in their seventies looked as good as my father did. What was his secret? Genes, maybe, since he didn't exercise or diet, and he kept a candy drawer, drank a pot of black coffee every day, and read in the middle of the night. Still, he took such joy in being a dad– and in life in general–and his happiness showed.

Jennifer Grant on her father, Cary Grant

Catherine Ledner

52, photographer, New Orleans, Louisiana, USA

My father, Albert, is one of the most amazing people I know. I'm biased, I know, but he really is amazing. He doesn't see things the way other people see things. He's ninety-one, a modernist architect of some renown, and is still working. He's an inventor too.

He was born in New York, but moved to Shreveport, Louisiana, as a baby. As a young child, he moved to New Orleans, where he still lives. His father sold furniture and his grandfather had the general store and post office in St. Rose, Louisiana, near New Orleans. That family was amazing; I've read things about what they did there.

Dad started doing modern archi- tecture in New Orleans when there really wasn't a lot of modern architecture. He went to Tulane University and studied with Frank Lloyd Wright. He was inspired by Lloyd Wright, but he was very much his own architect. It's so interesting that, having grown up in New Orleans, where the architecture was super Victorian, he developed the way he did, and created things and sees things so differently. He hasn't traveled or ever been to Europe.

After a while, he got a lot of recognition for his houses. He built the National Maritime Union headquarters in New York and later did two more buildings for them. One is now the Maritime Hotel in Chelsea. They are iconic because there is nothing else like them in New York.

He worked all the time when I was a child. He's still working—he's renovating a house built as a church

at the moment. He had a studio that was in the back of our house. He was always home, but he was in the back working. I could bring him things, and one of my favorite memories is of making him cookies and bringing them upstairs to his studio with a cup of hot cocoa on cold days.

I was a wild child. New Orleans fit me perfectly because it's a wild kind of place. Mom was an actress when she was younger, so I remember going to plays, and my dad was very much a supporter of her and her acting. It was a very colorful upbringing, and they sent my two older brothers and me to a colorful school. Dad and Mom led by example, by how they lived their lives with goodness and kindness and integrity. In so many ways, that really had the biggest influence on me.

They let us make our own decisions. There weren't a lot of rules, partic- ularly for me, as I was the third child. We weren't on our own, but we made a lot of decisions ourselves. They let me live my life how I wanted to and experiment in ways that many parents would have strongly objected to. They were both very open. There wasn't prejudice in our house.

I started taking pictures as a teenager, strange still-lifes. Later on, I decided that was what I wanted to do. And Dad's very proud of me— very much so.

When my son, Winston, was born I lived at home for a year. And then I rented a house a mile down the road. Later, when we'd moved to Los Angeles, Dad taught me how to step away when my son entered into young adulthood; how

not to overwhelm or pressure him. He taught me to let him make his own decisions and face whatever consequences those actions had.

Dad's a total optimist, always. Hurricane Katrina in 2005 was really hard. His house, his own creation, on the 17th Street Canal, was flooded when the canal breached. But after Katrina he came back to New Orleans and rebuilt his house. It's not exactly the same—the studio has gone—but it's very close. He saw it as an opportunity and he was one of the first to move back in after the hurricane. Then my mom passed away; that was really hard on him at the end. Now he lives there by himself and I visit about six times a year.

Interestingly, my best memories with him are being made now. I'm making a documentary about him and his designs with my cousin Roy. We've filmed in New Orleans and we'll go to film his projects in New York. I've learned a lot about him in the process and we've got to spend time together.

He was always home, but he was in the back working . . . one of my favorite memories is of making him cookies and bringing them upstairs to his studio with a cup of hot cocoa on cold days.

Awkward Conversations

Have you ever noticed how parents can go from the most wonderful people in the world to totally embarrassing in three seconds?

Carter Kane in Rick Riordan's *The Red Pyramid*

I wanted to ask my father about his regrets. I wanted to ask him what was the worst thing he'd ever done. His greatest sin. I wanted to ask him if there was any reason why the Catholic Church would consider him for sainthood. I wanted to open up his dictionary and find the definitions for faith, hope, goodness, sadness, tomato, son, mother, husband, virginity, Jesus, wood, sacrifice, pain, foot, wife, thumb, hand, bread, and sex.

"Do you believe in God?" I asked my father.

"God has lots of potential," he said.

"When you pray," I asked him. "What do you pray about?"

"That's none of your business," he said.

We laughed.

The narrator in Sherman Alexie's "One Good Man"

It's a very rewarding experience. It's mentally cleansing. It's like washing dishes, but imagine if the dishes were your kids, so you really love the dishes.

Chris Martin

I could have asked my father lots of questions. I could have. But there was something in his face and eyes and in his crooked smile that prevented me from asking. I guess I didn't believe he wanted me to know who he was. So I just collected clues . . . Some day all the clues would come together. And I would solve the mystery of my father.

Benjamin Alire Sáenz, from *Aristotle and Dante Discover the Secrets of the Universe*

In high school, when a boy would call and my dad happened to answer, he'd yell upstairs, without even covering the receiver, "Sarah! There's some mouth breather on the phone for you!" When my first boyfriend drove me to our first formal dance, and all the parents were taking pictures beforehand, my dad pulled my boyfriend aside, put his hand on his shoulder, and said, "Andy, keep your eyes on the road and your hands on the wheel." And it worked. The kid was too scared to slow dance.

Sarah Brown

Late Notes

Utah-based dad Seth King regularly writes imaginatively awkward notes to his children's schoolteachers and posts them on Instagram

Please excuse Isabella for her tardiness. We, as a family, had a difficult time this morning casting roles for our 2.m. production of "The Sound of Music". She wanted the role of Captain Von Trap and clearly she would be a better Brigita.
Thanks. ♥ Seth King

Please excuse Sophia for being late We were up late last night making our halloween (All Hallows Eve™) costumes and preparing our musical numbers/dramatic scenes to go with them. We are going to all be Cats from CATS: The Musical™ and in lieu of saying 'trick-or-treat' we shall grace each house with a snippet of that one-of-a-kind, long-running Broadway musical. Our neighbors are in for a treat; errrr... a musical treat!
Tender Hugs,
Seth King
#IWANTTOBEMAGICALMRMESTOPHOLES
#SOPHIAPRETENDSTOHATEHERPARENTS
#WEARESUPERHIP

Please excuse Isabella for being late. We were up late celebrating Columbus Day. In honor of the day we (as a family) went across our street to the neighbors house, occupied it, and claimed it as our own. We had a blast; although our neighbors weren't exactly "thrilled", LOL. When we let them back upstairs after having locked them in their basement we had a little explaining to do.
Hugs,
Seth King
#reallifehistorylessons #worldsworstholiday
#buyingagiftbasketfortheneighbors

Please excuse Carson for being late this morning. He was busy writing a song about rainbows for his grandmother, then he braided his sisters hair and baked us all cinnamon rolls. He's an angel.
#teenageboys Hugs, Seth King

Please excuse Isabella for being late. But maybe she wasn't late... maybe YOU were early. Maybe the concept of time only exists in our minds so we as humans believe something drives us forward outside ourselves... Hmmmmmm.

Seth King

Please excuse Nolan for being late. He was rummaging through his Dad's music collection and decided that N.W.A.'s "Straight Outta Compton" was a good choice for music to start his day. We had to have a very frank discussion on 'school appropriate' and 'school inappropriate' words.

Hugs,
Seth King

#straightouttaterrimancrazyfirstgradernamedNolan
#hesstinkingsmartyeahhisbrainsallswollen
#doeshishomework #notaschooljerk
#hisfavoritedancemoveisadeepsquatslowtwerk

Rapped to the cadence/song 'straight outta compton' first stanza.

Please excuse Sophia for being late. She was trying to shove almonds into the paper shredder to make homemade Almond butter... unsuccessfully. She refuses to eat anything processed after watching the documentary "FED UP™" due to the "hidden amounts of sugar in everything"... Alas, we appreciate her health-minded intensity.

Hugs,
Seth King

#SOPIAISSUGARFREE
#Sethnotsomuchbuttrying

Please excuse Carson for being absent. He was with his wildly popular boyband "Essence of Pubescence™" in the studio putting the finishing touches on their Irish-themed, St. Patty's day-centric album. Some of the featured songs:

• "You Lepre-conned My Heart"
• "Pot O' Cold" (AKA Post Break-up)
• "You're Me Lucky Charm"
• "Let's Darby O' Chill"
• "Finnegan's Wake... Board"
• "Choco Milk In the Jar" (to the tune of "Whiskey in the Jar")
• "Top of the Mornin' to You"
• "Just Pinch Me" (AKA Not Wearing Green on Purpose)

They are hoping to get the album released before the Irish holiday so it was a necessary recording session. Hugs, Seth

#blueeyesthatharmonize #Irishrootsarestrongwiththisone #O'Boyle.RULES

Dear Charles . . .

I have just had a letter from Aunty
Joan asking whether you received a
Christmas present from her. As in other
matters of life, you are childishly
idle about writing letters, thereby
giving the impression that you are both
ill-mannered and ungrateful. If people
bother to give you a present, the least
they can expect is that you rouse
yourself from your customary state of
squalid inertia and write and say thank
you. I am very fond of you but you do
drive me around the bend.

Roger Mortimer to his son
Charles at boarding school, 1969

Wait 'til your father gets home.

Every mother, ever

My darlings . . .

The dream of every family is to live happily together in a quiet and peaceful home where parents will have the opportunity of bringing up the children in the best possible way, or guiding and helping them in choosing careers and of giving them the love and care which will develop in them a feeling of security and self-confidence.

Nelson Mandela in a letter to his daughters, Zindzi and Zenani Mandela,

written on Robben Island, June 1, 1970

Mpho A. Tutu van Furth

53, episcopal priest, Cape Town, South Africa

I was born in England. We returned to South Africa when I was about three years old. South Africa was so different.

A few years ago, I was with my father in the Eastern Cape. As we went past this park in East London, my dad said, "You wanted to go and play in there and I had to tell you no. And you said 'Why?' I had to tell you that it wasn't for children like you." He had the challenge of having to explain apartheid to a three-year-old. I think that it was confusing to me. I couldn't see the difference between those children and me. They were just children playing in the park. They were children like the friends I had had in England. I couldn't figure out what it was about them that was so different . . . As I think about it, and as I think about the people whom I have come to call friends over the course of my life, I would have to say that, whatever it was that he said or however it was that he explained it to me, I didn't walk away having written off a race of people for the stupidity of some.

I am an episcopal priest. I studied and was ordained in the United States. When I got to seminary, I found out that my father was ubiquitous: he'd written the foreword for this text, the afterword for that text, and he was quoted in another text, and his speech is excerpted in yet another text.

I'm not sure whether it was a pain or an inspiration. It was a curiosity. I think I had taken him much more lightly than was warranted. I think that as I engaged in my own theological studies, and found him quoted and excerpted all over the place, I recognized him as much more of a heavyweight than I had given him credit for.

He wears his accomplishments very lightly. He's not the person who is constantly hammering you over the head with his achievements and what he's managed to do against the odds. He doesn't assault you with what it is that you have to live up to; that is not at all who he is. He was incredibly respectful of my process. He let me find my way, the way I needed to. When I told my mother that I wanted to go to seminary and I wanted to become a priest, my mom was a mom: she was thrilled and enthusiastic and excited. My dad prayed with me.

The day that I graduated from seminary at the Episcopal Divinity School in Cambridge, Massachusetts, my father was the commencement speaker at Virginia Theological Seminary in Alexandria, Virginia. He had agreed to the engagement before he knew my graduation date. I was really disappointed that he wasn't going to be with me, but I had made peace with it. My mom was going to be there and that was wonderful. He called me the morning of my graduation to apologize again and I was trying to be really fine, although I wasn't really, really fine. I didn't want to make him feel bad, because he was doing what he had to do. At the beginning of the ceremony, all the graduates marched in and then we were all seated. Suddenly I heard a small rush of

sound like waves on pebbles. I turned around and my dad was getting into the seat next to my mother. She was as surprised as I was. He had made his speech and jumped off the podium, run to a waiting car, got a flight to Boston, got a police escort from the airport to the chapel to come and be at my graduation.

He's not just a father: he is a daddy. He says so.

When my older sister celebrated her fiftieth birthday, my father and I celebrated the Eucharist. We had shared the liturgy before, but on those times one of us was preaching and the other presiding. This time we presided together and for me it was lovely—more than lovely. It was amazing and sacred and wonderful and all of those things. But afterwards I had an additional piece of context. I had a conversation afterwards with Brigalia Bam. She had argued for the ordination of women at the provincial synod that finally decided to ordain women to the priesthood in South Africa. She spoke about how important that was. She and others talked about how hard my father had worked for women's ordination and how he had prayed for it. She said, "He never knew when he was struggling for the right of women to become priests that one of the outcomes would be that he would one day be able to stand at the altar with his own daughter and concelebrate the Eucharist." That, in retrospect, made the moment even more momentous.

He had the challenge of having to explain apartheid to a three-year-old.

Parental Guidance Recommended

Give yourself permission to dream. Fuel your kids' dreams too. Once in a while, that might even mean letting them stay up past their bedtimes.

Randy Pausch

I have found the best way to give advice to your children is to find out what they want and then advise them to do it.

Harry S. Truman

My Dear Son . . .

If you can't win the scholarship, fight it out
to the end of the examination.

If you can't win your race, at least
finish—somewhere.

If your boat can't win, at least keep
pulling on your oar, even if your eye glazes
and the taste of blood comes into your throat
with every heave.

If you cannot make your five yards in
football, keep bucking the line—never let
up—if you can't see, or hear, keep plugging
ahead! Never quit! If you forget all else I
have said, remember these two words, through
all your life, and come success or failure,
I shall proudly think of you as my own dear son.

And so, from the old home-life, farewell,
and Godspeed!

John D. Swain to his son as he began student life

at Yale University, 1908

I'm in politics not in spite of the fact that I have kids, but because of the fact that I have kids, and they keep me really grounded in, "Well, am I doing things that are meaningful, or am I just sort of playing the game?"

Justin Trudeau

Now, Jack,

I don't want to give the impression
that I am a nagger, for goodness knows
I think that is the worst thing any
parent can be, and I also feel that you
know if I didn't really feel you had the
goods I would be most charitable in my
attitude towards your failings. After
long experience in sizing up people I
definitely know you have the goods and
you can go a long way . . . It is very
difficult to make up fundamentals that
you have neglected when you were very
young, and that is why I am urging you to
do the best you can. I am not expecting
too much, and I will not be disappointed
if you don't turn out to be a real
genius, but I think you can be a really
worthwhile citizen with good judgment and
understanding.

Joseph P. Kennedy Sr. to his son

John at boarding school, 1934

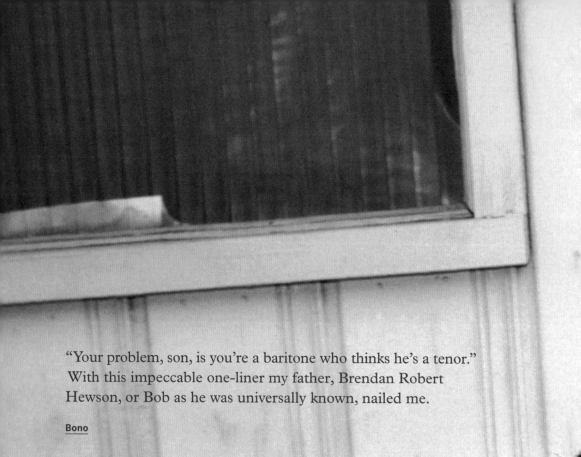

"Your problem, son, is you're a baritone who thinks he's a tenor."
With this impeccable one-liner my father, Brendan Robert
Hewson, or Bob as he was universally known, nailed me.

Bono

When I was a boy of fourteen, my father was so ignorant I could hardly stand to have the old man around. But when I got to be twenty-one, I was astonished at how much the old man had learned in seven years.

Mark Twain

If

If you can keep your head when all about you
Are losing theirs and blaming it on you,
If you can trust yourself when all men doubt you,
But make allowance for their doubting too;
If you can wait and not be tired by waiting,
Or being lied about, don't deal in lies,
Or being hated, don't give way to hating,
And yet don't look too good, nor talk too wise:

If you can dream—and not make dreams your master;
If you can think—and not make thoughts your aim;
If you can meet with Triumph and Disaster
And treat those two impostors just the same;
If you can bear to hear the truth you've spoken
Twisted by knaves to make a trap for fools,
Or watch the things you gave your life to, broken,
And stoop and build 'em up with worn-out tools:

If you can make one heap of all your winnings
And risk it on one turn of pitch-and-toss,
And lose, and start again at your beginnings
And never breathe a word about your loss;
If you can force your heart and nerve and sinew
To serve your turn long after they are gone,
And so hold on when there is nothing in you
Except the Will which says to them: "Hold on!"

If you can talk with crowds and keep your virtue,
Or walk with Kings—nor lose the common touch,
If neither foes nor loving friends can hurt you,
If all men count with you, but none too much;
If you can fill the unforgiving minute
With sixty seconds' worth of distance run,
Yours is the Earth and everything that's in it,
And—which is more—you'll be a Man, my son!

Rudyard Kipling

My friend was homesick and
got letters from his parents.
His mom's was two pages long.
His dad's just said, "Be a man."

Jimmy Fallon

He promised us that everything would be OK. I was a child, but I knew that everything would not be OK. That did not make my father a liar. It made him my father.

Oskar Schell in Jonathan Safran Foer's *Extremely Loud and Incredibly Close*

He was a better person than I am and I am not just saying this to appear modest. My father was one of those people who was born with a great sense of responsibility, far greater and more developed than mine. From the very moment he started going to school, he was a hard worker, very conscientious. I wasn't like that.

Aung San Suu Kyi

By the time a man realizes that maybe his father was right, he usually has a son who thinks he's wrong.

Charles Wadsworth

My father was my inspiration. He taught me that nothing comes without hard work, and demonstrated to me what hard work meant as a shift worker with two jobs. He taught me to be passionate about fairness. He taught me to believe in [the Australian] Labor [Party] and in trade unionism. But, above all, he taught me to love learning and to understand its power to change lives.

Julia Gillard

I wanted to teach my daughter the same things I had to unlearn after years spent as a corporate lawyer: that soul is more important than money, that love means more than material things.

James Griffioen

Parents rarely let go of their children, so children let go of them. They move on. They move away. The moments that used to define them–a mother's approval, a father's nod–are covered by moments of their own accomplishments. It is not until much later, as the skin sags and the heart weakens, that children understand; their stories, and all their accomplishments, sit atop the stories of their mothers and fathers, stones upon stones, beneath the waters of their lives.

Mitch Albom, from *The Five People You Meet in Heaven*

Desiderata

Go placidly amid the noise and haste, and remember what peace there may be in silence.

As far as possible without surrender be on good terms with all persons.

*Speak your truth quietly and clearly; and listen to others, even the dull and ignorant;
they too have their story.*

*Avoid loud and aggressive persons, they are vexatious to the spirit.
If you compare yourself with others, you may become vain and bitter;
for always there will be greater and lesser persons than yourself.*

*Enjoy your achievements as well as your plans. Keep interested in your career,
however humble; it is a real possession in the changing fortunes of time.*

Exercise caution in your business affairs, for the world is full of trickery.

*But let this not blind you to what virtue there is; many persons strive for high ideals;
and everywhere life is full of heroism.*

*Be yourself. Especially, do not feign affection. Neither be critical about love; for in the
face of all aridity and disenchantment it is as perennial as the grass.*

Take kindly the counsel of the years, gracefully surrendering the things of youth.

*Nurture strength of spirit to shield you in sudden misfortune. But do not distress
yourself with imaginings. Many fears are born of fatigue and loneliness.*

Beyond a wholesome discipline, be gentle with yourself.

*You are a child of the universe, no less than the trees and the stars;
you have a right to be here.*

And whether or not it is clear to you, no doubt the universe is unfolding as it should.

*Therefore be at peace with God, whatever you conceive Him to be, and whatever
your labors and aspirations, in the noisy confusion of life keep peace with your soul.*

*With all its sham, drudgery and broken dreams, it is still a beautiful world.
Be cheerful. Strive to be happy.*

Max Ehrmann

Marc Ellis

44, sportsperson and entrepreneur, Auckland, New Zealand

I am an only child, so for me, as a kid, my dad was part Superman, part soothsayer and 100 percent my best friend.

Chris Ellis was born in July 1942 in New Zealand. He lived in Melbourne, Australia, till about age seven, I think, and then lived in Wellington, where my parents raised me. He had an upbringing in a more traditional time, when there wasn't a lot of emotion shown. His father would come home, eat dinner alone. They'd give him a kiss on the cheek before going to bed and that was as much as they got emotionally. He was able to sit back and witness what he didn't have growing up and then make sure he gave it to me.

His father never came and watched him play sport, but Dad didn't miss any of my games. Every Saturday, we'd go and get out of the house while Mum had a sleep-in. We'd go boot a ball around for two or three hours at the park and get a Sparkling Duet on the way back from the shops.

He had a huge amount of energy then. I had my kids ten years later in life than he did and I'm not sure I have the energy he had. There were probably times he didn't want to get off the couch, but he always did.

That's part of the challenge of having an only child, I guess. I remember him making me a trolley because I loved trolleying. One day, despite having no practical abilities, he spent hours adding a back axle with some springs on it. He cut his hands to bits. I'll never forget him doing that, because it didn't come naturally.

My old man's always had a healthy disrespect for authority. He's principled. And he's a peacock—his dress sense veers on the side of costume. When he'd come to my school rugby games, he'd dress like he'd just come off the ski slopes in a one-piece red après-ski suit with a crocheted woollen hat and matching red moon boots. He had never skied a day in his life! It was my first taste of playing sport under extreme pressure.

There were photos on the wall at home when I was a kid of him in his Speedos, in a pose with the heading "Mr. Wellington 1982," which was funny when I was eight but pretty awkward when I was fourteen, and girls would come around and say, "Why's your dad such a dick?" But I think it reflects his joy for life, his enthusiasm and humor.

He gave me two bits of writing at two important stages of my life. There was "Desiderata" (see page 137) when I started university. He said, "Live your life by this and it will be a good life." Still to this day, I pick it up and read it. "If" (see page 129), by Kipling, he gave me when I was in my early thirties. But his best advice was, "If it feels good and it doesn't hurt anyone, do it."

I don't think there's been a time when he's been most proud of me. That's the cool, consistent thing about it. The worse it gets, the more he's got my back. And it's unconditional. That's the uniqueness of the bond between parent and child. If you have a dad who gives you that security of knowing there's someone in your corner, that's pretty unique.

One day soon, though, that will go. He and my mum have been living in Auckland, where I live, for ten years. Dad and I catch up for lunches; he likes a cold beer and a couple of oysters. We'll grab lunch together, talk about business, family. But he won't be in my corner forever. Recently he said, "I'm starting to feel my age because all my mates are dying." That must be a pretty ordinary situation.

By the time they get to a certain age, they've seen it all. I'm thankful for what my parents have given me, and while I'm not an overtly religious person I say a prayer every night, part of which is for me to look after them as they've looked after me. The tables do turn and you hope you can repay their kindness for many, many years, with patience and time.

imprint of Penguin Publishing Group, a division of Penguin Random House LLC.; page 76: from *The Letters of Samuel Beckett, Volume 1, 1929–1940* by S. Beckett, M.D. Fehsenfeld, L.M. Overbeck, G. Craig and D. Gunn (ed), Cambridge University Press, 2009; page 79: copyright © Guardian News & Media Ltd, 2016; page 81: from *Sons + Fathers: An Anthology of Words and Images*, Penguin Random House UK, 2015; page 83: from "What I've Learned: Iggy Pop" by Cal Fussman, *Esquire* magazine, March 2007, reprinted by permission of Hearst Communications, Inc.; page 90: copyright © David Sedaris, 2009, first published in *The New Yorker* and reprinted by permission of Don Congdon Associates, Inc.; page 91: Paul Rudd, reprinted by permission of the author; page 93: Maryum Ali, reprinted by permission of the author; page 95: from "Georgia May Jagger: Growing Up I Never Knew My Parents Were Famous—Dad Was a Musician, Mum Was a Dork" by Paul Thompson, *Daily Mail*, November 24, 2009, reprinted by permission of Solo Syndication; page 96: from "My Dad, Cary Grant" by Jennifer Grant, *Parade* magazine, May 1, 2011, reprinted by permission of *Parade* magazine; page 101: from *The Kane Chronicles: The Red Pyramid* by Rick Riordan, text copyright © Rick Riordan, 2010, reprinted by permission of Disney / Hyperion Books, an imprint of Disney Book Group, LLC., all rights reserved; page 102: from "One Good Man," in *The Toughest Indian in the World*, copyright © Sherman Alexie, 2000, used by permission of Grove/Atlantic, Inc., and any third-party use of this material, outside of this publication, is prohibited; page 104: from "Chris: I'm So Nappy," *The Sun*, July 9, 2008, reprinted by permission of News Syndication; page 105: from *Aristotle and Dante Discover the Secrets of the Universe* by Benjamin Alire Sáenz, reprinted by permission of Simon & Schuster Books for Young Readers, an imprint of Simon & Schuster Children's Publishing Division, all rights reserved; pages 108–9, Seth King, instagram.com/latenotes, used by permission of the author; page 112: from *Nelson Mandela By Himself: The Authorised Book of Quotations* by Sello Hatang and Sahm Venter, copyright © Nelson R. Mandela

and The Nelson Mandela Foundation, 2011, reprinted by permission of PQ Blackwell Limited, pqblackwell.com; page 124: from *Sons + Fathers: An Anthology of Words and Images*, Penguin Random House UK, 2015, reprinted by permission of Penguin Random House UK; page 128: Jimmy Fallon, twitter.com/@jimmyfallon; page 129: from *Extremely Loud and Incredibly Close: A Novel* by Jonathan Safran Foer, copyright © Jonathan Safran Foer, 2005, reprinted by permission of Houghton Mifflin Harcourt Publishing Company, all rights reserved; page 133: attributed to Charles Wadsworth, original publisher unknown; page 135: from "Long Live the Weeds and the Wilderness Yet" by James Griffioen, in *Things I Learned About My Dad (In Therapy)*, Kensington Publishing Corp., 2008, reprinted by permission of the author; page 136: from *The Five People You Meet in Heaven* by Mitch Albom, copyright © Mitch Albom, 2003, used by permission of Hachette Books, all rights reserved.

Image credits as follows: cover/spine: shutterstock.com/Dubova; pages 2, 4 (top & bottom), 15, 17, 18–19, 24–25, 26–27, 35, 44–45, 49, 50–51, 52–53, 56–57, 60–61, 68–69, 72, 77, 78–79, 80, 82–83, 92–93, 94–95, 97, 106–7, 118–19, 123, 124–25, 130–31 and 140–41: Getty Images, gettyimages.com; pages 6 (Viktorija Vaisvilaite Skirutiene), 31 (Davi Russo), 32–33 (Pietro Sutera), 46–47 (Graham Monro), 63 (Lisa Maksoudian), 74–75 (Genevieve Fridley): PQ Blackwell Licensing Limited, pqblackwell.com; pages 8, 21, 41, 65, 85, 99, 115 (image by Andrew Zuckerman), 139: copyright © the individuals featured; pages 4 (center), 38–39, 102–3: StockSnap, stocksnap.com; pages 12–13: tumblr.com; pages 36–37: Ruth Coward, pjslifestory.blogspot.co.nz; pages 58–59: David Laferriere, kritzels.com; page 71 (top): flickr.com; page 71 (bottom): Creative Market, creativemarket.com; pages 88–89: instagram.com/fashiondads_; pages 108–9: Seth King, instagram.com/latenotes; pages 112–13: Matthew Willman, used with permission of The Nelson Mandela Foundation, nelsonmandela.org; pages 132–33: Gallery Stock, gallerystock.com.

First published in the United States of America in 2017 by Chronicle Books LLC.
First published in New Zealand in 2016 by PQ Blackwell Limited.

Concept copyright © 2016 by Marc Ellis and Kirsten Matthew
Design and layout copyright © 2016 by PQ Blackwell Limited

Library of Congress Cataloging-in-Publication Data available.

ISBN 978-1-4521-6162-4

Manufactured in China by Everbest Printing Co. Ltd

PQ Blackwell
Publisher: Geoff Blackwell
Editor-in-Chief: Ruth Hobday
Designer: Matthew Moss
Editorial and research: Rachel Clare
Additional editorial: Kimberley Davis, Benjamin Harris, Leanne McGregor

All acknowledgments for permission to reproduce previously published and
unpublished material (including photographs) can be found on pages 142–3.

10 9 8 7 6 5 4 3 2 1

Chronicle Books LLC
680 Second Street
San Francisco, California 94107
www.chroniclebooks.com